ONE COMPANY, UNDER GOD

Simon S. K. Lee
EIS Office Solutions, Inc.

ONE COMPANY, UNDER GOD

ONE COMPANY UNDER GOD

1st Edition

To order additional copies of this book, contact:

EIS Office Solutions, Inc.

(877) 557-7300

orders@eisoffice.net

> He prayed, "O LORD, God of Israel, there is no God like you in all of heaven and earth. You keep your covenant and show unfailing love to all who walk before you in wholehearted devotion.
>
> 2 Chronicles 6:14 (NLT)

DEDICATION

To my Lord and Savior, Jesus Christ, whose death on the cross paid the price for my sins and whose ascension from the grave sealed my victorious eternal life. Lord, I am forever in debt for Your love and sacrifice. This book is written to honor Your name with the hope that others will see how magnificent and loving You are. Thank you for Your grace that continually washes away my sins and provides me with second chances.

I also thank Christ for healing me of a speech impediment, depression, and suicidal thoughts. It is through His healing power that I am here today. Thank you Jesus for all you have done in my life. This book is dedicated to You and You

alone!

TABLE OF CONTENTS

Dedication iv

Table of Contents..................................2

Foreword..4

Acknowledgments 5

Introduction...7

The Mission Field 9

My Testimony 21

The Dream 31

The Journey 42

Obstacles and Challenges......................54

Leadership and Teamwork.....................65

Love of Money and Power......................78

It is all about God..................................91

Future Vision.......................................101

Life is Short..109

Works Cited 113

Footnotes...115

FOREWORD

The words caught in her throat as tears welled up in her eyes. Faye, soon-to-be-bride of Simon Lee, could not get the rest of her sentence out. All eyes of our short-term mission team were on her as we debriefed our week in Panama.

Seated by her side was Simon, who began to "translate" her tears to the rest of us. He told us that she was filled with joy from our work there giving hope to people. She nodded "yes." He told us she wanted to say she had received way more than she had given. Her emphatic nod again confirmed Simon was accurately interpreting her tears.

That was my earliest memory of Simon and Faye Lee. Many people are good story-tellers. Simon and Faye are great story-doers. They live out what they believe.

This book is for the first-time entrepreneur, as well as the experienced exec--anyone who wants to bless people as much as make a profit. In these pages you will learn from someone who accomplishes both. Be prepared to be challenged as you read.

Mike Jorgensen
Executive Director, I am Second

FOREWORD

ACKNOWLEDGMENTS

I praise God for my parents, who moved our family from Taiwan to the United States to provide us with a brighter future. It was here that I met Jesus Christ, my Lord and Savior. I praise God for my parents who work tirelessly and love me so much. Their example and work ethic in establishing a successful business has allowed me to do what I do today. God has used both my mom and dad to bless me tremendously. I want to thank them both from the bottom of my heart.

I also wish to thank the four pastors who have mentored me throughout my life: Pastor Andrew Gackle, my middle and high school pastor; Dr. and Pastor David Daniels, my college pastor; Pastor David Hsu, my pastor from ages 23 to 38; and my current Pastor, Dr. Peter Swann.

Pastor Andrew, you taught me so much at such a young age about what it is like to follow Jesus with full abandon. Your dedication to and love for Jesus Christ will forever remain a great example to me.

Pastor Daniels, thank you for sharing your love for the Word of God and your passion for discipleship with me. I will always remember the blessings I received when you shared your words of great wisdom with me at the Union. I praise God for you, the one who planted a deep passion in my heart for the Word of God.

Pastor David Hsu, thank you for showing me what it takes to successfully lead a large organization with a servant leader's heart. I learned so much about servant leadership from you. The way you love people and sacrifice your time for the sake of the church offers great encouragement to me.

Pastor and Dr. Peter Swann, thank you for loving me and the people around you so much. It is your love for God and for His people that has changed my life forever. Thank you for demonstrating strong theology and the power of God in such a balanced view. It has challenged my walk with God. Thank you!

Last, but definitely not least, my wife and life partner for the last ten years. Without her support and love, my life's work would not be possible. I still remember explaining to her when we first got married that I would not be taking a salary from EIS for the first two to three years after it started. You can imagine what most women would have said. Her response? "I did marry you for the money, but I married you." Thank you, Honey, for all your prayers and support over the years. I love you so much!

ACKNOWLEDGMENTS

But people who long to be rich fall into
temptation and are trapped by many foolish
and harmful desires that plunge them into ruin
and destruction. For the love of money is the
root of all kinds of evil. And some people,
craving money, have wandered from the true
faith and pierced themselves with many
sorrows.

I Timothy 6:9-10 (NLT)

INTRODUCTION

What if . . .

- ➤ Corporations were more concerned with transforming lives than pleasing stockholders?
- ➤ Business owners cared more about helping people than exploiting people to maximize profit?
- ➤ God was present in the Board room?

Imagine the lives that could be transformed around the world!

This was God's vision for our company, which He established in 2003.

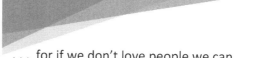

... for if we don't love people we can
see, how can we love God, whom we
cannot see?

I John 4:20b (NLT)

THE MISSION FIELD

The following statistics are meant to challenge each one
of us to consider what God might be calling us to do for His
people:

Wealth

*The total wealth of the world's three richest
individuals is greater than the combined gross
domestic product of the 48 poorest countries – a
quarter of all the world's states.[1]*

*40% (the equivalent of $165 million worth) of
the food produced in the United States ends up
as trash. **

*Some 1.1 billion people in developing countries
have inadequate access to water. 2.6 billion
people lack basic sanitation. [†]*

"More than a quarter of all the water that is used worldwide is taken to grow a billion tons of food that nobody ever eats." [‡]

Endangered Children [§]

- In the United States 400,540 children are living without permanent families in the foster care system.
- Around the world, an estimated 153 million children have lost one parent.
- 17,900,000 children have lost both parents, live in orphanages or on the streets, and are at risk for disease, malnutrition, and death.

Homelessness

- On any given night in the United States, anywhere from 700,000 to 2 million people are homeless.
- 3.5 million people (1.35 million children) will experience homelessness in any given year.

Human Trafficking

Every night on streets all across America, children – babies, really – are forced to perform despicable sexual acts in an explosion of the sex slave trade, headquartered right here in Houston, Texas!

What is God's Plan?

While making money is not easy, giving it away is even harder.

In answer to a young rich man's question about what he had to do to go to heaven, Jesus responded that the young man would have to give up all of his possessions and follow Him. Mark 10:21 (NLT) talks about how difficult it was for the rich man to give away his material things:

> *"Looking at the man, Jesus felt genuine love for him. 'There is still one thing you haven't done,' He told him. 'Go and sell all your possessions and give the money to the poor, and you will have treasure in heaven. Then come, follow me.'"*

Then Jesus said to his disciples, "I tell you the truth, it is very hard for a rich person to enter the Kingdom of Heaven."

Don't misunderstand! God does not ask us to give away all of our material things in order to be saved. But this passage affirms Jesus' statement. The young man could not put the things of heaven before his material wealth. When given the choice, the rich young ruler chose to turn away from serving Jesus rather than give up his material wealth.

The critical question is this: If we lose everything – our house, car, even the ones we love – will we still worship God?

The answer to this question will expose the truth. Do we worship God or things that are ephemeral?

Even more importantly, if God is asking us to sell everything and follow Him, will we be willing do it? I know so many people whom God has called to serve the poor or go on overseas mission trips, but they cannot because they are so trapped by materialism and the love of money. The death and resurrection of Christ demands that we give up everything for His glory. We are either all in or all out!

Every company is in business to make money, and Christian businesses are no exception. There is nothing wrong with wanting our businesses to be successful. In fact, if a company does not make money, it will cease to exist. However, Profit is not the enemy; *greed* is.

Too many Christians model their businesses after non-Christian counterparts, with financial success being their *primary* goal. I Timothy 6:10 (NLT) warns that "*...the love of money is the root of all kinds of evil.*" The temptation to seek personal wealth instead of God's Kingdom can be overwhelming if we do not pray about and establish a financial plan that includes how we will use the profits we expect to generate.

One thing we need to make sure we are clear about is that fancy cars and big houses are *not* the sin Scripture talks about. Instead, it is the **love** of money. It is the never ending **desire for** material things and money to satisfy our empty heart. If Jesus does not even have a place to lay his head, how much more do we really need to satisfy our soul? There should be a point in our lives – as CEO's or not -- that full satisfaction must come from Christ and Christ alone.

Expanding God's Kingdom by increasing company profits can go hand-in-hand if the company's financial plan takes into account how to invest future profits. Later in this chapter, we will explore this topic more in-depth.

Some people believe that it is wrong for Christian businesses to compete side-by-side with major chain stores in terms of size and annual profits. They argue that the desire to make sizeable profits is somehow wrong for Christian businesses. Not so!

What God will consider is how a company *uses* the wealth it accumulates. 2 Corinthians 9:5-7 (NLT) tells us:

> *"So I thought I should send these brothers*
> *ahead of me to make sure the gift you promised*
> *is ready. But I want it to be a willing gift, not*
> *one given grudgingly.*

*Remember this—a farmer who plants only a few
seeds will get a small crop. But the one who
plants generously will get a generous crop.*

*You must each decide in your heart how much
to give. And don't give reluctantly or in response
to pressure. 'For God loves a person who gives
cheerfully.'"*

God honors the charitable giving of companies just as
He honors charitable giving by individuals.

When we talk about giving, some people feel negative
feelings toward this act of obedience. Giving is considered a
sacrifice. However, Scripture reminds us that giving is so much
more. Giving is a reflection of our heart. It is a true test of what
our heart is longing for.

The more we love money, the more we long to keep it.
We want to be in control of it. We believe money does not
belong to God; it belongs to us. So, giving is a very good
barometer of what our heart truly longs for.

However, when we love giving money away to expand
God's Kingdom, we long for God's blessing. We want to give it
to God. We believe money does not belong to us; it all belongs
to God.

God loves a cheerful giver. Scripture reminds us in Philippians 4:13 (NLT): "... and my God will provide all of your needs according to His riches in glory. . ."

The key word here is "needs." We have far more desires than needs. In Mark 6:30-33 (NLT) God promises us:

> ". . . if God cares so wonderfully for wildflowers that are here today and thrown into the fire tomorrow, He will certainly care for you. Why do you have so little faith?
>
> So don't worry about these things, saying, 'What will we eat? What will we drink? What will we wear?'
>
> These things dominate the thoughts of unbelievers, but your heavenly Father already knows all your needs.
>
> Seek the Kingdom of God above all else, and live righteously, and He will give you everything you need."
>
> Mark 6: 30-33 (NLT)

What a powerful reminder of God's faithfulness in our lives.

The question is not whether God wants us to use company profits to expand His kingdom; the question is *how* much we should give away. Many Christian companies give ten percent of their money away, and that is a good start. However,

Biblical giving is not based on a percentage or a specific dollar amount; it is based on our faith and trust in God.

My recommendation is to give away an amount that is faith-based, not just convenience-based. Does the amount we choose to give allow us to trust God more, or does it allow us to trust ourselves more? We should give an amount that reflects our full faith in God. When we ask God in faith how much we should give, God will answer. If the amount we give is too small, we are probably not listening to God's voice. Listen to God and God will honor your request.

If God says to give five percent, we will give away five percent. If God wants us to give away one hundred percent, we will give away one hundred percent. Again, it is not so much about how much we give, but more about being faithful to the call that has been placed before us.

Not all of God's businesses will make a profit. God establishes nonprofit corporations to solve social problems. Their purpose is completely different from that of a Fortune 500 company. Nonprofit corporations are uniquely equipped by God for the work they are called to, not for making a profit. But solving societal problems can cost a small fortune. Research and development alone can be in the millions of dollars. How can they see their mission through with no income?

WHO IS GOD CALLING?

If we are Christian entrepreneurs, then regardless of our stock ownership, we own nothing in our companies. God owns everything. We do not even own a one percent share of our company. God owns 100 percent. Until we get this right, we will always think we are in control. God is in control, and we must let Him be in control. This starts by understanding that God owns everything and that He is allowing us to use it in the name of Jesus, in order to bring glory to the Kingdom of God.

There is a tendency in Western culture to try to separate our personal lives from our public lives. What we do at home is our personal life, and what we do at work and when we go away from our homes is our public life. Both lives are gifts to us from God. How we handle them is our gift back to God.

Where we can run into trouble is when we think we can live either our public or our private life apart from God. We must live both lives with integrity and consistency. We should surround ourselves with likeminded Christians who will hold us accountable both at home and in public. It does not matter whether our actions can be seen by one or many here on this Earth; we are ultimately responsible to God.

I lose count of how many times the Bible refers to the Pharisees as hypocrites. They look good on the outside; but on the inside, they are full of sin and corruption.

The question is this: "Have we one hundred percent surrendered our lives to Christ?" If we have, then God not only owns one hundred percent of our lives, but also one hundred percent of our companies.

> *"For all the animals of the forest are mine,*
> *and I own the cattle on a thousand hills."*
> *Psalms 50:10 (NLT)*

As with having a plan for our lives, He also has a plan for our companies to succeed. While we may not understand it, we are part of a strategic partnership much larger than our businesses alone. God is calling Christian businesses to become financial partners with His nonprofit corporations.

As we get ready for Christ's second return, it is critical that we get this right. If not, we will be wasting the very breath that God has granted us. God is calling all Christian business people from around the world to take up the call of the Great Commission.

Matthew 25:29 (NLT) is the foundation upon which EIS Office Solutions was established.

> *"For whoever has will be given more, and they will have an abundance. Whoever does not have, even what they have will be taken from them."*

> Matthew 25:29 (NLT)

We invest fifty percent of our corporate profits in eleven local and worldwide missions, and God has faithfully continued to grow the business of EIS Office Solutions. Why? Because God knows we are passionate about giving money to the least of His children. It is our calling, and we love every step of our journey with God. We are so grateful to run a company not just for profit, but to see lives change.

Although we sell over 50,000 kinds of office supplies and office furniture, that is not our calling. Our calling is to donate our profit so we can see God change lives around the world.

I hope the following chapters will inspire you and encourage you to see what a great CEO God is when we let Him run our lives and our companies.

QUESTIONS FOR REFLECTION

1. What mission field(s) has God called you to?

_____

_____

_____

_____

2. How have you responded to that call?

_____

_____

_____

_____

3. If you have no mission field yet, what do you think is stopping you from allowing God to work through you?

_____

_____

_____

_____

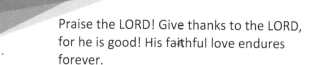

Praise the LORD! Give thanks to the LORD, for he is good! His faithful love endures forever.

Psalms 106:1 (NLT)

MY TESTIMONY

I was born in 1974 in Tainan, Taiwan and am the son of a third-generation entrepreneur.

Tainan is one of Taiwan's oldest cities and cultural capitals. Known for its rich folk culture and thoughtful preservation of local rites and traditions, numerous historical monuments – including the first Confucian school/temple, built in 1665, and the original Eastern and Southern gates to what is known as the "old city" – remain beautifully preserved to this day. Tainan also claims more Buddhist and Taoist temples than any other city in Taiwan.

When I was just five years old, my family moved to Taipei, the capital of Taiwan, and my dad started Shang Shin Trading Company. My dad was an extremely successful entrepreneur. He would go out of his way to ensure a smooth business transaction. I remember him learning Arabic so he could do business in Saudi Arabia. My dad was adventurous and focused on his business.

Though the business in Taiwan was extremely successful, my dad wanted to venture out and give our family a better life in the United States. In 1983, at the age of eight, I moved with my family to Houston, Texas.

The move was extremely difficult for me. Not knowing English and starting from scratch learning the ABC's offered plenty of opportunities for my classmates to make fun of me. I remember in seventh grade when a boy named Mark took my glasses and broke them in half. I was so furious that I turned around and punched him between the eyes. I left him unconscious for a few minutes, and both of us were subsequently suspended from school for three days. I remember that incident as if it were yesterday, not because I knocked him out or because we got suspended from school but because of the beating I received when my parents found out I had been suspended! The beating was a lesson I will never forget.

While in Taiwan, we had attended the local Buddhist temple on holidays and special occasions and we worshipped our ancestors as was expected in the Asian culture, but we were not "religious" in my opinion. I was quite surprised when my parents accepted an invitation to visit Tallowood Baptist Church here in Houston shortly after leaving our Asian motherland.

I was thirteen when my parents shared their decision to accept Christ and they asked me if I would like to join them. As I recall, their explanation of baptism was that you got to get "dunked." As a teen, I thought being dunked sounded fun, so I went along with this "family" salvation experience.

The problem, however, was nothing in my life changed. I was still a struggling, rebellious teenager who cussed at church and did everything I could to avoid going. I saw church in America like I had seen attending the Buddhist temple in Taiwan – as a social function.

The true turning point in my life came when I was sixteen. I had been invited to attend a youth group retreat, which again sounded like a great social outing. There were about sixty teenagers in attendance one night when my pastor asked the group, "If someone were to walk through those doors right now with an AK-47, would you be willing to stand up for Christ?" I remember clearly that everyone in the room except my cousin and me stood up, and I sat frozen in my chair. I just wasn't ready to admit that I needed Jesus in my life.

The next night, the speaker gave the same invitation. He knew that there were two of us who had not accepted the invitation the night before. Had I gone forward the night before, I would have been repeating my earlier "family" salvation experience. I would have just been going along with the crowd. This night I was not part of the crowd. This time I was the only one standing.

Standing alone that night, salvation became a life-changing reality for me. I went instantly from "unsaved" to "on fire for Christ." Trashing everything that reminded me of my old life, I relinquished complete and total control to God.

It was the first time in my life that I understood who Jesus was and who I was as a person. Up to this point, I had believed that the purpose of religion was to allow people to do good because being good was the only way one could go to heaven.

That night I realized that my life was not good and that no one on earth is good. We are all sinners. We all make mistakes. No one is perfect. Heaven is a place of perfection, and no one can enter heaven by their own power. Jesus Christ came down from Heaven two thousand years ago and died, not just for my sins, but for the sins of everyone everywhere in the world.

All of my sin during my rebellious teenage years, all of my present sins, as well as all of my future sins were all forgiven when Jesus Christ died on the cross and arose victoriously three days later. Not only did Christ die for our sins on the cross, but He conquered sin in our lives so that we are now able to live victoriously.

Jesus Christ is like no other. He lived a perfect life. No one else in history can claim that. He remained sinless, without hatred, until His death on the cross.

Look at the leaders of the world religions. Look at the person who founded them. Is he or she worth living and dying for? What kind of person founded the religion? How does he or she compare to the person of Jesus Christ?

There is not and has never been any other person like Jesus. His love extravagant, his forgiveness eternal, and his life extraordinary, he sacrificed heaven to come down to earth to die a death that He did not have to so that we could all experience true love and forgiveness. It was an act of courage and deep love. Jesus Christ is the one worth living and dying for, and that day, I gave my life to Christ. I was no longer in control; I fully surrendered my life to Him.

My life radically changed at the age of sixteen. I remember my youth pastor, Andrew Gackle, who openly lived a life of abandonment to Christ. Pastor Gackle exemplifies a life that is fully surrendered to Christ.

I remember asking him how much he made serving as youth pastor at our church, and I was shocked to know how little the church was paying him. Pastor Gackle had to teach English on the side to make extra income, but he never complained. He drove a beat-up car which our youth group called "Old Faithful" because he had to pray each time he turned the key or it would not start!

It is one thing to trust Christ, but it is another thing to see Christ's love in action through the life of a person. Pastor Andrew Gackle showed me at a young age what love with abandon looks like. I praise God for this man.

In 1993, while attending the University of Texas, I joined the campus ministry Chinese Bible Study (CBS). During my senior year, I was honored to serve as its president. CBS eventually grew to be the largest Christian organization of any kind on the UT campus. I look back almost twenty years later; this was where God planted the leadership seed in my life.

It was during my college days that my faith grew the most. College is a defining moment for many students. Their faith either grows by leaps and bounds or it dies by the wayside. Sadly, most students fall away from their faith the minute they enter college. They choose a life of drunkenness and partying. I thank God for protecting me from all that. Through my Bible study group, church, and accountability group, God used various tools and events to protect me and cultivate my faith.

I remember going to First Evangelical Free Church in Austin and listening to Pastor David Daniels. My first reaction to hearing him speak as a young freshman was I could not believe that the Word of God could be so fun to read yet so applicable in life. One of the main reasons I attended Dallas Theological Seminary shortly after college graduation was because of the impact this man made by bringing the Word of God to life.

I still remember the analogy Pastor Daniels made about the Word of God. He asked how many of us would get mad when we drive on the mountainside where there are guardrails on the roads to protect us from falling down the canyon. In fact, we would feel the complete opposite and be delighted to be protected by the guardrails. Scripture is the guardrail to life. It protects us from falling deep into our sin. We ought to be grateful that God gave us this wonderful book. When I heard that illustration from Pastor Daniels, my world and view of scriptures just turned upside down. I looked forward to going to church every Sunday to hear how the Word of God can transform our lives.

My first experience serving on a mission trip was a trip to East Asia in 1994. While there, I had the opportunity to play a short pick-up basketball game with a student from a local university. It seemed odd to me that he played in a pair of old dress shoes. Needless to say, his footwear offered no competition for my Air Jordan athletic shoes, and I beat him quite easily. Later, when I asked why he wore dress shoes to play basketball, he replied that those dress shoes were the only pair of shoes he owned.

That one brief comment rocked my world!

Never in my wildest dreams would I have imagined someone on Earth only owning one pair of shoes. In my young adolescent life, I was only surrounded by material goods and the comforts of life. I never experienced having so little in my life so it was extremely shocking to witness someone living without the many amenities in life that I had always viewed as being necessary. Little to me maybe, but to this student, he was grateful to own even one pair of shoes.

My paradigm on material things shifted greatly that day. God planted a seed in my life of contentment that is still with me today. How much we have does not matter; what does matter is being content, and from there, experiencing true joy in this life.

QUESTIONS FOR REFLECTION

Take time right now to write out your testimony.

1. When, where, and how did you accept Christ as your Savior?

_____

_____

_____

_____

2. Since accepting Christ as your Savior, name one (or more) amazing thing He has done for you.

_____

_____

_____

_____

_____

_____

_____

After the wise men were gone, an angel of the Lord appeared to Joseph in a dream. "Get up! Flee to Egypt with the child and his mother," the angel said. "Stay there until I tell you to return, because Herod is going to search for the child to kill him."

Matthew 2:13 (NLT)

THE DREAM

After my first mission trip to East Asia, God prompted my heart to dedicate at least one time a year to an overseas mission trip. I believe God really wanted me to go outside of the comforts of the United States and experience what real suffering was like. At the same time, I was blessed to share the greatest story ever told – that of the Lord, Jesus Christ – with people who have never heard of him before.

From 1995 to 2010 God provided a way for me to visit numerous poverty stricken countries including Kenya, Panama, East Asia, Bolivia, Peru, Russia, South Sudan, and Mexico. God had been using these trips to chisel away at my selfish desires. Over the years, my old desires to be wealthy, comfortable, and powerful were slowly but surely disappearing from my life, replaced by new desires to become a servant, giver-of-wealth, and lover-of-the-least-of-these. Please don't get me wrong. I still struggle with materialism and the love of money from time to time, but it no longer has a grip on my life. I give thanks daily for the transforming power of God's grace and love.

In 2003, I returned from a life-changing mission trip, but this time, something was different. I didn't slip right back into life as I had always known it. Instead, I found myself lying in bed one night, unable to sleep. When I did eventually sleep, I would dream of the number 50 in neon lights. As the dream repeated night after night, I began to wake up whenever the number 50 appeared. This happened for 30 days straight. One night when I awoke, I got out of bed, dropped to my knees, and asked God, "What do You want from me, Lord? Why do I keep seeing this number 50?"

I knew God had equipped me in the area of business because of the intense satisfaction and enjoyment my work provided. I was confident the number 50 had something to do with my future as a businessman; I just didn't know what.

It seemed clear after approximately three months of prayer and consultation with mentors, pastors, and friends that God was calling me to start a company.

By this time, I had been working for my dad's company as the president of sales and marketing for seven years. I had no plans to start my own company.

This was troubling for me because in Asian culture, if a family owned a business, the oldest male in the family would take over the business when his father retired. It was never openly discussed; it was just understood.

A son could bring shame on his family and opt out of his responsibility, but that was never my attitude. As the oldest male and a third-generation entrepreneur, my goal to follow in my dad's footsteps had been settled when I was very young.

Business is in my blood as it has been with my father and his father. My dad and I had it all planned. I would attend college, work a few years in the corporate world, work with my dad's company for a while longer, and then take over the company when he retired.

Even more confusing was the specific number "50." I was positive God was calling this new company to donate the unheard of 50 percent of its profits to His Kingdom. I was willing to do the work, but my business training and experience both asked "how"?

I have never wanted to become wealthy or accumulate material things. Instead, I haveto be purposeful in the way I do things. I did not want to waste time or quality of life chasing after a certain dollar amount on a paycheck.

My parents had taught me to live conservatively. Whenever I was considering making a big purchase or spending a large sum of money, they would remind me, "Live conservatively, Son. Don't buy it if there is no need for it." You could say saving money and not wasting was a part of my DNA.

At the time of these dreams, I was working for my dad as the vice president of sales and marketing. When I walked into my dad's office and shared with him that I felt a calling from God to leave his company and start a new one, he was shocked. His immediate response was that I must be mistaken.

I told him that there was no way I could ever dream this idea up on my own. After all, I was quite happy with things as they were. But, I really wanted to use my gifts and talents to help change this world for God's glory.

Scripture tells us to honor our parents. Yes, I could have made the choice to rebel, to turn my back on my father and his wishes and just start my own business. But I had a second option – one God would honor – to allow time for my parents to pray about this important decision and for God to work in all of our hearts.

My ad and I left that first discussion agreeing to pray – dad with my mom and me with my fiancée – about this matter. We did not have repetitive discussions about the topic. Instead, we spent time apart, praying and seeking God's advice.

My parents loved Jesus. I knew that they would obey God's calling, not their own. I knew that if this is indeed God's calling in my life, God would speak to my dad and mom, too, and they would obey Him, regardless of how painful obedience might be for them.

A couple of months later, my father walked into my office bearing a check for $50,000. I thought it was my year-end bonus because it was not unusual for it to be that large, but it was not my year-end bonus. Instead, dad said he was giving this money to help me start EIS Office Solutions, Inc.

Tears ran down my face as I realized what God had done. Not only were my parents supporting me, they were giving up their own dreams of seeing their only son take over their company. Recognizing the enormous sacrifices they were making for me, I dropped to my knees and thanked God for His love and grace. God had used that time of prayer to change my parents' hearts! As a result of following God's plan, EIS began business in 2004 with my parents' blessing.

I firmly believe that dreams[**] and visions[††] are ways God speaks to all believers. We miss out on blessings from God when we miss His dreams and visions. God told Moses:

> *"Hear now my words: 'If there is a prophet among you, I, the Lord, make myself known to him in a vision, and I speak to him in a dream.'"*

> *Numbers 12:6 (NLT)*

When we do receive a dream or a vision, the vision is always accurate. It is how we interpret and make that dream come true that is important.

I hear people say all the time: "God told me this, so I'll do it." But sometimes when God tells us to do something, it's not very specific, like my number 50. How that is interpreted and how that plays out is sensitive. Love is indeed patient. It will not be rushed. Unless God tells us that we need to do something on a specific date, we must take time to make sure we understand the interpretation. The dream or vision must play out in God's timing.

Dreams may foretell either good or evil. Just as God speaks to us through dreams and visions, Satan uses nightmares and dark, sinful, lustful dreams to torment us. We have all experienced nightmares. So it is important before we sleep to pray and ask God to cover us with His dreams. I have always asked God to speak to me this way.

Scripture makes it clear that in the end times, God will speak to young men and women in dreams.

> *"'In the last days,' God says,*
> *'I will pour out my Spirit upon all people.*
> *Your sons and daughters will prophesy.*
> *Your young men will see visions,*
> *and your old men will dream dreams.'"*
>
> *Acts 2:17 (NLT)*

Each night I begin with a request for God's protection from the evil one. Then, I ask God to speak to me through dreams. Some are clear and others are vague, but all are recorded in a journal. I pray constantly over my dreams, asking what God wants me to do with each one. Because every dream from God is important, I never want to neglect or forget one.

God can speak through people, His word, or directly to us. I have practiced being sensitive to God's voice. We must take time to be sure we understand the dream, verifying our conclusions through Scripture, Godly counsel, and circumstances. However, once we are sure we know what the dream means, we must act quickly. Whatever God asks of us, we must be faithful to carry it out.

So many people come to me and say they have had dreams, but they don't carry them out. Either they're scared or they just don't know how to do what is being asked of them, so they end up wasting a dream or a vision. When God gives us a dream or vision, carry it out. God is going to use us for His kingdom, and dreams are just one way He does that.

If we do not act on the call of God, our ears will become dulled and God will choose not to speak to us in the future. God knows that we will not obey, so He will not let His name or His call be mocked.

EIS Office Solutions evolved from a dream to a company that, ten years later, is able to support seven nonprofit organizations in the Houston area. We are passionate about giving money to the least of God's children. It is our calling, and we love every step of our journey with God. We are so privileged to be able to run a company not just to profit, but to see lives changed!

QUESTIONS FOR REFLECTION

1. What dream(s) has God laid on your heart?

    _____
    _____
    _____
    _____

2. What factors are critical to realizing God's dream(s) in your life or business?

    _____
    _____
    _____
    _____

3. What miracles would it take for you to begin God's dream for your business or life?

    _____
    _____
    _____

_____

4.   What proof can you give from the Bible for your
     answer?

     _____

     _____

     _____

     _____

5.   Give an example of where God has already done a
     miracle in your life or business.

     _____

     _____

     _____

     _____

6.   How did that make you feel?

     _____

     _____

     _____

     _____

7.   What specific action can you take today to begin to
     realize God's dream?

_____

_____

_____

_____

"Owe nothing to anyone—except for your obligation to love one another. If you love your neighbor, you will fulfill the requirements of God's law."

Romans 13:8 (NLT)

THE JOURNEY

According to the Wall Street Journal, three-fourths of all venture-backed business startups fail. [‡‡] In addition, an article from Mashable reports an even higher ninety percent failure rate for technology startups. [§§]

When we talk about the life process of a journey, many entrepreneurs love the end result of the journey. They are just not willing to do what is required to get there.

I believe there are two measuring sticks for success – the one used by the world and the one used by God. These are vastly different units of measurement.

The world's measure of success is all about revenue and profit –often leaning more toward the profit side.

The measure of success within a Christian company does not involve profit at all; it is about being faithful. Are we being faithful in *all* things, big and small?

When EIS was a struggling business, we tried to cut corners to save money. For instance, we considered using one software license for all users instead of buying multiple software licenses.

The Lord quickly convicted us about sacrificing our core values in order to achieve a predetermined end result. In the eyes of God, the end result for our Christian company was not a bottom line, but a moral line. The Lord stopped us from following the path of the world. Romans 13:7 (NLT) instructs:

> *"Give to everyone what you owe them: Pay your taxes and government fees to those who collect them, and give respect and honor to those who are in authority."*

The way we treat our colleagues is a significant core value at EIS. When Jesus was asked which commandment was the greatest, He replied:

> ". . . 'You must love the LORD your God with all your heart, all your soul, and all your mind.'
>
> This is the first and greatest commandment.
>
> A second is equally important: 'Love your neighbor as yourself.'"
>
> Matt. 22:37-39 (NLT)

We have no "employees." Everyone who works for God at EIS is a "team member," and are all treated as part of the EIS family.

Everyone at EIS gets a one month paid vacation from day one. They do not have to accumulate it or work for it. Our work hours are 9:00 a.m. to 4:30 p.m., and we take two hours to go to lunch together on Fridays. EIS pays for lunch twice each month.

The reason we do this is because working people to death for the sake of profit is not the overarching goal. We want to treat everyone as team members but, more importantly, we respect their lives outside of work. In fact, we tell our team that their lives outside of work are overwhelmingly more important than their lives at work. If that is true, then we should allow people to take time off from work, to go home early, and to create a place where people enjoy going to work, rather than just working for a paycheck.

Those who hold leadership positions at EIS lead as servant leaders. This is a subject I will cover in greater detail in a later chapter, but Luke said it like this:

> *"But among you it will be different. Those who are the greatest among you should take the lowest rank, and the leader should be like a servant."*
>
> *Luke 22:26 (NLT)*

As servant leaders, we are willing to work side-by-side with every team member, united in our commitment to achieve success within God's plan.

The initials in our name stand for "E" – Excellence, "I" – Integrity, and "S" – Selflessness. We uphold these values.

As Christians, we strive for excellence in all that we do. We expect all of our team members' actions to be a direct reflection of "God with skin on." Any time we encounter another person, whether colleagues or customers at work or our spouse or children at home, they should see Jesus reflected through our speech and our actions.

While it is difficult to say which Biblical principle is most important, a big one at EIS is integrity. The "I" in EIS stands for "integrity." We do not lie. We do not lie to customers. We do not lie to each other. Lying is one thing we just do not do around here. Integrity is a huge part of the journey. To have core values is crucial to a Christian company.

It may be tempting to lie to a customer and tell them an order was misplaced or lost. However, we do not do that at all – not to a vendor, not to a customer, and not to each other. We only hire people who have high core values.

Finally, the "S" in EIS stands for "selflessness." There is nothing that is "not my job." Everyone pitches in to get the work accomplished. If one team member is overwhelmed at the same time another team member has a lighter load, we expect the available team member to help out without being asked.

The success of a Christian company will come from that company's faithfulness, and the results will speak for themselves. Whenever a Christian company is successful, God is glorified.

END RESULTS

We are all humans, and humans make mistakes. As a Christian company, it is very important that we balance giving grace and making strong business decisions. The Apostle Paul reminds us that we live in grace, but we should not take advantage of grace. We have had to let team members go from our company because of either theft, lack of cooperation, or lack of adherence to the culture of the company. We will usually work with team members and give them up to three chances. If we don't see improvement, unfortunately, we have to let them go. I learned from the beginning that it only takes one uncooperative team member to destroy the culture of a company.

With that being said, our interview process is much stronger than ever before. Using a DISC*** profile, doing two layers of references, and other testing, we have been very successful at hiring solid team members who understand the company's culture and are willing to work hard to get us there.

"S" stands for "Selflessness." We enter this world as very selfish individuals. It is in our DNA. Babies quickly learn to communicate their needs and wants, and they think they are the center of the universe. As parents, it is our job to teach our children that they are not the center of the universe, and neither are we. God is ultimately the one who is in control, and we want our children to understand that at a young age.

It is nearly impossible for a company to grow if each individual is looking out only for their own best interests. Teams make companies successful, not individuals. Each morning the members of our team are invited to gather together and spend fifteen minutes praying and encouraging one another. If anyone has gone beyond their job description to help other team members out, we acknowledge that teamwork the next morning. Following through and emphasizing our core values over and over again will result in everyone buying in. Merely posting our core values of "Excellence, Integrity, and Selflessness" on the walls of the office but not holding anyone accountable to them would be completely useless.

Are there times when we are faithful yet the results are not what we would like? Yes. But, God did not call us to produce results. Results are up to God. He called us to be part of His plan, His journey, and to be faithful each and every step of the way. If we have been faithful to the Lord throughout the journey, the end will be a resounding success in God's eyes.

Have there been times when I have wanted to give up? Yes. But the thing about a vision from God is that God tells us when to start, and God tells us when to end. The times when things were not going the way I might have wanted and I wanted to end the journey, I always realized that God had not told me to stop yet. Therefore, I kept going.

I have seen companies change their vision because they did not like the preliminary results. The vision of a company should never change. The vision needs to stay the same because it is the reason why they exist.

Even though the vision is permanent, the *process* can be changed. How we get to the vision is critical. Many leaders fail to know the difference between the process and the vision.

The process can be changed over and over. In fact, if something seems to be failing, a small adjustment in the process may be the key to success.

For example, our company's vision is to donate fifty percent of our profit to God's work. At times, this giving really puts a strain on our cash flow. Does this mean we need to change the vision? The vision was given by God. Did he make a mistake? Hardly.

The process of how we give that money away can be adjusted. Instead of giving all the profit at the end of the year, we can divide that giving into four times out of the year. We still fulfill our commitment, but it puts less strain on the cash flow.

This is exactly how we figured it out. The process was what needed to be change and not the vision.

It is so important that we follow God during good times but even more so through bad times. It all comes back to faithfulness. We are almost ten years into this company, and I can tell you that if I hadn't persevered, if I hadn't trusted the Lord, if I had not stayed focused on Him, this company would have closed a long time ago.

QUESTIONS FOR REFLECTION

1.   Where are you on your spiritual journey today?

_____

_____

_____

_____

2.   What do you want to change?

_____

_____

_____

_____

3.   When will you make that change?

_____

_____

_____

_____

4.   How is the success of a business measured in God's
        Kingdom versus the world's view??

_____

_____

_____

_____

5.   How are you currently measuring the success of
     your business or life?

_____

_____

_____

_____

6.   If you currently have a business, what is your
     Mission Statement??

_____

_____

_____

_____

7.   What are your core values?

_____

_____

_____

_____

8.   What are your core values for your personal life?

_____

_____

_____

_____

Then they cried to the LORD in their trouble, and he delivered them from their distress.

Psalm 107:28

OBSTACLES AND CHALLENGES

Many companies write books or talk about themselves, and they usually focus solely on their successes. But, the truth is, all companies experience a natural up-and-down curve of growth and decline. One good month does not represent "success" any more than one bad month means "failure." Success just happens to be easier to accept and share than failure.

At EIS Office Solutions, God is the head of this company. He is our CEO. Whether we ultimately achieve success or failure, God will always be with us. Whether times are good or bad, God never leaves us. He is running the company behind the scenes, and we make decisions on behalf of the company based on prayer and faithful execution.

In our third year in business, we were about to run out of money. In fact, we only had about a month's worth of cash left in the bank to sustain the company. I got down on my knees to pray, and I remember being really angry. I would have loved to say that I had great faith and trusted God through and through. But the reality of it was that I was scared, and I lost many nights of sleep. I would wake up early in the morning with sweat on my face because I was so scared that our company would tank. It didn't make sense that He would ask me to start a company and then set that company up for failure. What I didn't know was that God was really setting us up for success!

One week into my time of prayer, a company called Steve & Barry's University Sportswear contacted us to see if we would be interested in bidding for their business. They were asking us to bid against Staples and Office Depot for their nationwide contract which included over three hundred retail stores in the United States.

When asked why they were inviting us to bid along with two of the United States' major office supply companies, they responded that they had seen our story online and really wanted to give us a chance because they appreciated what we did with our profits.

We submitted our best possible bid on the Steve & Barry's University Sportswear contract. Two weeks later, we learned we had been awarded the contract worth $2.5 million a year! At that time we only had two team members. Overnight, we hired four or five new customer service representatives. Our usual two or three orders a day suddenly exploded to eighty orders a day! We couldn't believe what was happening.

When I looked back at that time, it pains me to recall how little faith I had and how frequently I doubted God. Even though I knew in the back of my head that God was going to take care of us and that He was still in charge, what had happened felt completely surreal.

Then in 2012, it happened again. We had been informed we were going to lose about forty percent of our business. Our top four accounts were not going to renew their contracts. These four large school districts in the Washington DC area were going to cancel our contract to buy local. My sales manager, account executive and I traveled to Washington DC in an effort to change their minds; but at the end of the day, they chose to buy locally.

Three months before that, I had been on my knees asking God, "What should I do?" During that three-month period of prayer – I believe in March of 2012 – I drove four and a half hours to Plano, Texas, which is a city near Dallas, to meet with a friend. We met in a little shack under I-45.

As we were eating, an elderly lady walking with a cane approached our table and proceeded to sit down without even asking us. I asked my colleague if she was a friend of his, but he shook his head.

Suddenly, she put down her cane and gently placed her hand on my arm. "Sir," she said, "you don't know who I am, but I believe I have been praying for you for the past two weeks. In my prayer, I saw someone like you."

My immediate reply was, "Ma'am, I'm not from Plano, Texas. I'm from Houston. I just drove up this morning to meet with my friend today."

"You don't understand," she continued. "I've been praying for you for two weeks. God gave me a specific message to deliver to someone. When I saw you, I knew you were that person."

Although I was shocked by her words, I shared with her that as a Christian, dedicated to serving Jesus Christ, I did believe that God spoke through people. Whatever she was going to tell me, I was open-minded and wanted to hear it.

Quietly, she shared, "God told me to tell you three things, young man. First, He wanted me to let you know that God has heard your cry."

My mind reeling, I shared with her that I had, in fact, been crying out to God for the last three months. At that moment, I still questioned whether her message was truly from God because that statement was very generic. She could easily have made it up. What little faith I had!

As I waited, she continued, "I have another thing to tell you. The second thing is that God is going to take care of your company."

It was at that moment that I knew without a doubt that this message was from God. The hairs on my arms raised and I literally began shivering. No one in that restaurant, including this kind woman, knew I owned a company. In fact, she had no way of knowing whether I even had a job. She said God was going to take care of my company. I started weeping tears of thanks, realizing that God was in total control over this company.

But, she was not done yet. There was still one more message left for me.

She then looked straight into my eyes and declared, "God will be giving your company its largest profit ever during the year of 2013."

"You know, we're about to lose forty percent of our business," I blurted.

"No, I didn't know that, but all I am doing is telling you what God told me to tell you," she replied.

> God is our refuge and strength, always ready to help in times of trouble.
> Psalm 46:1 (NLT)

Before she left, she laid her hands on me and prayed over me. I felt the love of God flowing into my body. In that moment, I began to really appreciate who God is.

God did not have to do that for me, but He did. He was so intimate with me. He did not have to use that woman to share with me. He didn't have to talk to me at all. He could have left me alone. I would have still trusted Him. But, He chose to do something extraordinary.

I drove home to Houston that day and could not wait to share this conversation with my wife. I also recorded it in my journal and added it to my Facebook page so everyone would know what God had done.

January 2013 rolled around, and with it, big expectations for the New Year. But when nothing really extraordinary happened for the next six months, I began to doubt. Our sales receipts were still going down. Nothing had happened.

Then, on July 1st, our sales manager rushed into my office and announced, "Simon, I have a lot of good news. First, we just won the State of Wisconsin contract."

I could not believe it! That contract covered the toner cartridge needs for all government offices in the state of Wisconsin. At the same time, we were awarded four other large contracts we had bid on. For good measure, a number of our contracts were going to be renewed that month, including one with the state of Mississippi. All of this business began flowing during the month of July. We had the best month ever – record profit, record revenue. When I reviewed the numbers again in

December, I found that the pattern had continued every month – record profit; record revenue.

These contracts were exactly what God had revealed to me through the lady I encountered in Dallas. It was all coming true. I thank God every day for His love for our company and for me. He is indeed running the show at EIS Office Solutions, Inc.

THE DIFFERENCE

When it comes to timing, I have learned that it is not about our timing. I am a Type A personality, and I want everything fast and now. Given my personality type, it is often difficult for me to allow God to work in my system. Nevertheless, God is more concerned about our devotion and love for Him than anything else. My relationship with Him meant so much that He sent His only Son to rescue us. I often look back and think: if God had answered my prayers my way, all of these lessons about life and who He is would have been for naught. It is through difficult trials like this that we can see the hand of God at work. God is the God of the impossible, and He alone controls the timing to display His magnificence.

The difference between a Christian-owned company and a Christ-owned company is dramatic. Many Christian-owned companies do not give control to God. Just a Christian-owned company could be a company that happens to have a Christian at the helm as CEO. In the case that the company is only "Christian" by name and not by heart, the CEO believes that he or she is in charge.

A Christ-owned company is completely different. Here at EIS, Christ is the owner and captain of the ship. He runs the show. We are simply waiting for Him to do His thing. That does not mean we're lazy. It does not mean as business owners, we do not do anything. We work as hard as we can. But at the end of the day, we trust God and God alone. Whether we experience success or failure, at the end of the day, it is all about Him.

QUESTIONS FOR REFLECTION

1.   What are some of the challenges that Simon faced?

_____

_____

_____

_____

2.   How were Simon's challenges like some you are currently facing or have faced in the past?

_____

_____

_____

_____

3.   Who or what do you turn to when things are going badly in your life or business?

_____

_____

_____

_____

4.   What do you fear in your life or business?

_____

_____

_____

_____

5.   What does Scripture have to say about your fear?

_____

_____

_____

_____

He sat down, called the twelve disciples over to him, and said, "Whoever wants to be first must take last place and be the servant of everyone else."

Mark 9:35 (NLT)

LEADERSHIP AND TEAMWORK

I personally believe there are two types of managers: servant leaders or dictators.

Some of us in our lifetime may have worked for a dictator. A dictator is not just someone who says "my way or the highway," but also a very insecure person who uses his position at work for his or her own security. I have talked to a few leaders like this in my days, and when you ask them why they think they need to impose their will and power over people, they will always tell you, "This is business. Decisions have to be made, and we don't have time to all get along."

I am not here to stir up a controversy, but there are many successful and profitable companies that are being run by "dictators". The company may be profitable, but in terms of the emotional health of those who have worked for the company, there have been some heavy casualties along the way. Employee turnover, job dissatisfaction, and words of anger left behind all speak of a highly dysfunctional team.

A company close by that I know of runs by that kind of a system. Some of my friends who worked there were expected to work overtime without pay whenever managers demanded them to. With over ten thousand employees, the company treats its employees more as slaves rather than as valued blessings. It is not surprising that turnovers are high and employee satisfaction is extremely low.

On the contrary, there is Google. We have all heard of Google. Their culture, the company's value of their team members, and long hours are highly publicized. One of the things that team members at Google say over and over is that they feel like they are part of the Google team. (Harvard Business School Case Studies, 2014). Teams work together and try their best to come to a consensus. Everyone's opinion is highly valued. In fact, most of the great ideas at Google came straight from their team!

In my opinion, the best example of a servant leader is Jesus Himself. Consider the responsibility He was given by God. Jesus bore responsibility for the sins of the entire world! However, in order to complete that unbearable mission, He exercised the power of the almighty kingdom of God. He had access to more power than anyone in the history of mankind.

Despite the power at His command, Jesus humbly stooped as a servant to wash the disciples' feet. The lesson taught through that one act of service was not meant just for the disciples; rather, it was a powerful lesson for all time and all people on the character of a true servant leader.

The reason I believe this lesson is so important is because very few Americans truly understand what it would be like to live in a dictator environment. In America, if we do not like our jobs, we can get a new one. If we don't like the current president, we could choose not to elect the same person next time. However, many other countries around the world do not have the luxury or freedom to choose their destiny. Growing up in Taiwan, I am very familiar with the power a dictator possesses. Before Taiwan had free election in recent years, presidents and officials would be tyrants to their people. There is absolutely no servant quality involved. No one in Taiwan at the time really enjoyed that.

Let me just say, I have never heard anyone who worked for a dictator say they enjoyed their job.

A positive working atmosphere is just one of the benefits that come with servant leadership. Jesus used the following illustration frequently:

> *"Whoever wants to be first must take last place and be the servant of everyone else."*
>
> *Mark 9:35 (NLT)*

The world, defines "success" quite differently:

> *"[t]he position of being more successful than anyone who you are competing against."* [†††]

Leaders in the world are taught to be all powerful, all controlling, and even to manipulate the situation if necessary.

Christian leadership is just the opposite. Life is not about what we can do; it is all about what God can do. He is in control in every situation, including leadership, and He will receive the glory when a company is led by a servant leader.

Even many Christian businessmen minimize the likelihood of a servant-led company achieving the same success as one that is led by a dictator. They say servant leadership has its place: in the church, in the family, and in marriage. But business is different. Whatever a leader says has to take place.

Decisions have to be made and, at the end of the day, the leader is the one who must make things happen.

I strongly disagree and believe most Christian businessmen get this part wrong. Servant leadership applies to all aspects of our lives: marriage, family, and business. Jesus did not instruct us to be servant leaders in just one aspect of our lives; He called us to be servant leaders in *all* things.

Jesus himself personified the dynamic of being all powerful while serving others. Service is not a sign of weakness, but actually one of power. When we think about the character of God, we should recognize that He was all powerful; yet, He was all loving when He gave His only Son as the sacrifice for our sins. Christian businessmen have to get this right. True power is embodied by servant leaders who train and contribute to the success of those around them.

Negativity is using power to suppress people. Positivity is using power to serve people. How does a servant leader share power with his team members? First and foremost, servant leaders understand that their power comes from God. Indeed, it is a gift from God meant for them to become blessings to others. For instance, a manager is entitled to make a decision at any given moment. However, that decision may be deferred to his or her team depending on the circumstances. If a team manager asks the manager a question, the manager can ask them for their feedback. This is just one out of many ways in which power can be shared with team members. I believe when team members see a powerful leader make the choice to serve others, they are even more inspired to give their best. He has just leveraged his power from negative to positive. When team members observe a manager serving them, they will recognize him as a great leader.

So how does this concept of servant leadership work from a practical standpoint?

The way in which decisions are made is one way EIS expresses servant leadership. Whenever a manager is facing a decision, he or she will either call the team together or personally talk with each one, seeking each team member's opinion on the decision at hand. The decision may not directly involve them, but we have learned that if we fail to ask team members to contribute, they will ask why we made a decision without considering them.

I always tell our managers to hear everybody out. Team members know that we may not always accept or use their opinion, but they are happy to be heard. At the end of the day, we cannot please everybody. Although it is a team, it is not majority rules either. Our decisions are always based on what is best for the company and its needs at that point in time.

We try to be sure everyone is heard, and we appreciate each and every opinion and suggestion our team members share with us. I can tell you as a fact that our team members appreciate having their opinions valued.

We tell our team members that no idea is a bad idea. Every idea is valid and is heard. This policy creates open dialogue between everyone so there is no single dictator deciding everything; decisions are a group effort. When everyone chips in, the team becomes more powerful.

When we stop valuing the opinions of team members, they will feel less inclined to share their opinions with us in the future. I know one worker who was directly asked for their opinion by his boss; and once he had reluctantly shared it, he was fired! How many employees do you think would share feedback with the company after hearing a fellow employee being fired for doing so?

Companies must improve and change for the better, or they will become stagnant. Change begins from the ground up. If team members stop sharing their opinions, things will not change. Management may not know what is going on at the ground level. The only way managers will know what changes need to be made is if team members are comfortable coming forward and sharing their opinions and suggestions with management.

To be servant leaders, we must be able to put ourselves in someone else's place. I have always appreciated when a company respected my time and could be flexible when needed.

An example of how we can serve our team members is offering flexibility when personal emergencies arise. Most of the time, the one month of leave our team members receive is sufficient to allow time to rest and relax with our family and to cover sickness and other personal days. But unexpected emergencies and tragedies occur that can force a team member to use more than one month of time off.

Begin by imagining what you would like the company to do for you if you have always been a loyal member of the team. You would want them to extend the time you need without adding a missing pay check to your worries.

At EIS, we view families as being more important than the company, and we try to work with team members during times of distress.

We also want our team members to be able to participate in school and church activities with their families, so our work day goes from 9:00 a.m. to 4:30 p.m. Everyone is out the door by 4:30 p.m. Many times, I am the first one out at 4:30 p.m. I really try to lead by example in this area! There are a few that stay past 4:30 p.m., and I try my best to acknowledge their hard work the next morning.

We not only value our employees' time with their families and respect their need for emergency time off, but we take our team members out for lunch every other Friday. We thank them for a job well done by taking them to lunch. Our team members really appreciate the fact that the owner of the company notices the effort they put in during the week.

TEAMWORK

Everybody at EIS Office Solutions works as a team. And when I talk about as a team, I mean we can all step in and cover for one another. Every team member, although assigned to one specific department, is cross-trained in all of the other departments. In that way, when one department needs help, everyone else can pitch in to assist them, and when someone is out for vacation, illness, or emergency, their job is covered with no loss of quality.

In many businesses, employees actually hide knowledge from other staff members because they don't want anyone to be able to do their job as well as they can. We work under the opposite philosophy. Every team member knows their job very, very well; but, when necessary, even a team member from a completely different department can step in to help out.

When I teach management, I first stress the importance of cross-training everyone. If your business uses a team philosophy, you should be cross-training all of your employees.

I also emphasize the *importance* of every member of the team. If one person is late, it affects everybody else. If one person is slacking off, it affects everybody on the team. It is critical for everyone to think as a team, not as an individual. In fact, one of the words that we do not use is "employees". Rather, we use the words "team member" The company does not own anyone. The company is made of team members who work together for the good of the company. Each one is valued and respected.

If you turn to the Gospels and study Jesus teaching the disciples, you will notice that He began with a team of twelve disciples, and He sent the disciples out as teams of two or three. Whenever a team is responsive to the needs of its members, whenever the team works well together, there is momentum;

things happen better and faster, and this is true for the company as well.

Whenever a team is positive, the individual is taken out. Everything becomes all about the team, and you have a dynamic working environment.

QUESTIONS FOR REFLECTION

1. How would you categorize your leadership style?

    _____

    _____

    _____

    _____

2. Does your leadership style reflect your faith?

    _____

    _____

    _____

    _____

3. How would your family or coworkers categorize your leadership style? Would they say they know you are a follower of Jesus through your leadership?

    _____

    _____

    _____

    _____

4. What are the characteristics of how Jesus led?

_____

_____

_____

_____

5.   Where do you need to be more like Jesus in your leadership?

_____

_____

_____

_____

6.   Where in your life or business are you trying to be first, rather than to be last and a servant?

_____

_____

_____

_____

> "No one can serve two masters. For you will hate one and love the other; you will be devoted to one and despise the other. You cannot serve both God and money.
>
> Matthew 6:24 (NLT)

LOVE OF MONEY AND POWER

THE LOVE OF MONEY

There is a reason why the subject of money comes up so frequently in the New Testament. Jesus mentioned several times that you cannot love money and God at the same time.

The love of money is the reason many people turn away from their faith and fail to follow God's plan, both in their personal and professional lives.

I want to reiterate that money is not the root of all evil; it is the *love* of money. How do we know if we love money? My college pastor told us that we can usually tell by looking at our bank account. What have we been spending and what are we giving away? This is usually a very accurate barometer of where our heart is.

It has been ingrained in my heart since I was a boy that money is not for pleasure or to accumulate material wealth; it is mainly to give away. Money can occasionally be used for pleasure, but that is not the primary reason why God gives us money as the pursuit of the finer things in life is how money gets us in trouble. God gives us money so that we can ultimately use it for him. One of the ways in which God directly refers to how money should be used is stated in the Scripture which says that if we don't provide for our family, we are worse than unbelievers. Because providing for our families is a Biblical mandate, it is one thing that is especially important to me. Occasionally taking my wife out to a fancy dinner and a nice vacation from time to time is a way I take care of my family and enjoy the money God has blessed me with without losing sight of what money is really there for.

Corporate America is bombarding us with the concept that bigger is better. The message seems to be that you will be happy if you get that Prada bag or the latest iPhone you will be the coolest person in town. We probably all know the person who says that last week's "bigger and better" thing is now "old," so they have to buy the newest "bigger and better" thing just to keep up with their insatiable thirst to get more. A love for money and the pursuit for materialism is a guaranteed journey to pure emptiness and greed.

I am reminded in Matthew 5:4 (NLT) that "blessed are the poor in spirit for they shall inherit the kingdom of God." The disciples in Chapter 4 of Matthew had just left their jobs and income to follow Jesus. Jesus is reminding them that you might be poor, but those are the ones who will have more in Heaven. Is Jesus calling us to be poor? By all means, no.

But let me ask you this: What if God allowed Satan access to you because He believes you, like Job, will still worship Him? What if Satan took everything away from you – job, home, vehicles, family – like he did Job? Are you going to worship God or despise Him? If God is calling us to be poor, are we still going to say that Jesus is enough for us?

As a six- to seven-year-old boy living in Taiwan, I remember having compassion for beggars walking the streets of the market. I felt so bad for them that I would beg my mom to give money or anything we could to them. My mom would have to drag me away saying, "Don't worry about it. They'll be okay."

That memory of knowing that those people would eventually be okay has remained with me throughout my life.

I also remember going to Kenya in 2003-2004, where I met kids on the street who had not eaten for weeks. They were nearly naked with maybe a pair of shorts to wear. I was 29 years old when I personally observed the devastation poverty wielded over the residents of third-world countries.

In their poverty, I remember a family in Nyeri, Kenya, who invited our team to their shack to have a cup of tea. It was most likely the only thing they had left to eat or drink. But, they offered it to us as a gesture of their kindness and hospitality. I cannot even use words to describe how humble I felt when they gave their best to us. I remember the poor woman who gave everything to Christ and how Christ said that was better than the rich man who gave only part of what he had. What a powerful reminder that God owns everything, and we need to just give our very best.

It is unbelievable to me how wealthy Americans are, even though we may not feel like it. I am one of them! The money we spend, the things we buy, and the number of things we think we need is disturbing compared to the poverty in the rest of the world.

We, as Americans, do give away a lot of money, but are we giving our best and giving it sacrificially or are we giving in to our comfort zones?

One thing I am very careful about is my salary, which is currently $40,000 per year. I did not pay myself the first two or three years after start-up, and my salary began at $24,000 in our fourth year of operation. By 2012, the company was growing, and I was making $50,000. However, I asked that it be reduced to $40,000 when the company lost some of its customers.

Money is a tool God gives us to use for our personal needs and to expand His kingdom. That is all. Nothing more and nothing less.

How did I choose $40,000? There were a few reasons. To protect myself from the love of money and to ensure my testimony would remain unaffected, I did not want to be the highest paid person in the company.

Also, if I tell people that our company gives half of its profits away but I take home millions of dollars in salary, it does not represent who God is in my life.

I believe God wants me to live a simple lifestyle. Jesus didn't own a large house. Jesus – the King of the Universe –

But Jesus replied, "Foxes have dens to live in, and birds have nests, but the Son of Man has no place even to lay his head."

Matthew 8:20 (NLT)

didn't own anything; yet, we own so much.

Another reason I chose that salary is because when God called me to start EIS Office Solutions, He very kindly provided additional income to care for my family. As a part owner of my dad's company, I receive a year-end bonus every year that helps our family out. This extra income God provides to care for my family has helped to affirm my belief that He was, in fact, making it possible for EIS to donate 50 percent of its profits to charity.

I was also conservative and saved money when I was single. So, at this time, financially, we are doing fine. This gives us a very fine line where we are trusting God with our finances at the same time protecting us from the love of money and the desire of wanting more and more.

It doesn't mean I can never receive a raise. It doesn't mean God can never bless me more financially. It just means we are doing well right now. If we add to our family or if a financial need should arise, obviously, there will be a reason to give myself a pay raise, but right now, there is no need.

I want to protect my heart from the love of money. I think too many Christian businessmen begin their businesses with the intent of representing the Kingdom of God, but they end up allowing money to control their hearts. It is so critical that we do whatever we can to protect ourselves.

I do believe in making money for our company because I believe that money can be a blessing to others. However, we do need to make sure as CEOs and presidents of Christian companies that we let people know how we are doing financially. Are we giving for God's glory? Or, are we living a lavish lifestyle desiring to satisfy our hearts where only God can fill the chasm of emptiness?

Worshiping God with our tithes and offerings is not just about maintaining a salary that is not extravagant; it is also about using money to bless others. In addition to our company donating fifty percent of its profits, my wife and I are blessed to donate another fifteen to twenty percent of our personal income as well. Donating and tithing are both part of protecting us from the love of money.

In this side of life, we will never know the impact our donation will be, but one day, God will graciously allow us to see the eternal impact we made not just with the giving but our lives as well. What a glorious day that will be when Christ will be honored through all the great things He has done through us.

Jesus told the rich young ruler to sell everything he owned and follow Him. But the love of money and materialism had become his gods, and the young man sadly walked away from following Jesus rather than give up everything he owned. One way to prevent money turning us away from Jesus is through regular giving.

As Christian leaders, we need to be held accountable to give for God's glory. Many leaders feel "no one should hold us accountable because we are the top," but that is contrary to the truth we find in the Bible. We all need to be accountable to God for our finances and how we spend our money. I frequently ask my brothers in Christ to ask me how I am doing in that area.

Giving away is not something that we do naturally or spontaneously, even though that can happen when we have been called by God. Most of us must give regularly until it gradually becomes an integral part of our lives. My family makes sure that we learn about the organizations we give to, how much we are giving, and why we have chosen to give. We talk it out as a family to make sure that regular giving takes place.

Another way I protect myself from the love of money is by remembering that I own nothing as everything belongs to the Lord. If someone has borrowed something from me or if someone needs something from me, I see it as blessing others with the wealth God has given to me. The simple act of paying for a meal or to meet a need is very important to me.

I think everything can be summed up this way: Do we really believe God owns everything in our lives, or do we think we are the ones who made it happen? Letting go is one of the biggest obstacles to following Christ. It is in surrendering and letting go that we find God. I promise you that heaven is much better than holding on for dear life. At the end of our lives, we are not going to take anything with us. We might as well practice eternity right now. Don't let the devil deceive us that we need to be in control of our money and our lives. God is in total control, and we just need to let God lead.

THE LOVE OF POWER

Why is power so addicting? We have seen great leaders in the past and present fall because of an addiction to power. When we are on the top of the world, we seem to be invincible.

Everyone looks up to us. Power feels great. That is why most of us fall into this trap.

It is so easy for us as CEOs to be in a position where we feel like we are on top of the world. As I mentioned earlier, we must be servants in all areas. When a leader is serving his team members, he is not striving for power. In a sense, that seems backward, but that should be a high priority for servant leaders. The higher your position, the more important it becomes.

Why is power so attractive? I truly believe power provides control for a leader. The leader feels like, not only is he in charge of his destiny, but the destiny of many. To be able to dictate the future and force people to follow is indeed an enticing temptation. In the beginning when God created the heavens and earth, the angels and God were in complete harmony. But, because an angel named Lucifer wanted to have power over God, he rebelled and many angels followed. This addiction to power has been with us since the beginning and it is one of the lies of the enemy. We should not be surprised when so many leaders fall into this trap.

So, what does serving your team members look like? Well, when something needs to be tended to in the office – whether it is cleaning the toilet or taking out the trash or helping team members out – if I have time, I will do it. If everyone feels that way, whatever we need will get done. So, don't ask people to do the work that you see in front of you unless you don't have time. That's a different situation. If you have time, go ahead and make it happen. Show servant leadership. Show that you're not in it for the power, but you are in it to serve.

There is no task that is too little for a leader to do. The moment we feel like we are beyond any task, it is time to reevaluate what kind of leader we really are.

Power has an addictive influence on everyone. As we serve more, the negative influences of power become less. From power comes pride, but we can combat pride through servant leadership. The more we learn about Christ in Scripture, the more Christ-like we should strive to become.

At the end of the day, what the world lacks is the ability to harness power with humility. We use all of the power that God has given us to serve and love. If we serve and love well, our company will change for the better and this world will change for the better. Scripture reminds us so well that we can teach, preach, and prophesy; but if we have not love, we are nothing. Love is the epitome of servant leadership. Jesus Christ lived this out so well. With all the power in the world, yet He chose to serve. He is the example we must all follow.

QUESTIONS FOR REFLECTION

1.   What is the central idea of this chapter?

_____

_____

_____

_____

2.   How did Simon tie into Jesus' Sermon on the Mount as it relates to money?

_____

_____

_____

_____

3.   Who in your life needs uplifting, either financial or personal encouragement, and could God be calling you to help?

_____

_____

_____

_____

4.   In what ways do you protect your heart from the "love of money"?

_____

_____

_____

_____

5.   What makes power so dangerous?

_____

_____

_____

_____

6.   Why does having power seem to be so addicting?

_____

_____

_____

_____

A man's heart plans his way, but the Lord
determines his steps.

Proverbs 16:9 (CSB)

IT IS ALL ABOUT GOD

Many decisions are made during the formation of a new business. In most cases, a business resembles its founder. This resemblance is reflected in the character of the business: its work ethic, organization, purpose, and so on.

The temptation is just as strong for Christian entrepreneurs to allow personal life experiences to influence the foundation of their businesses as it is for non-Christian entrepreneurs. The truth is, many CEOs who say, "We're all about customers," are really thinking more about themselves than their customers.

> *"...What do you have that God hasn't given you?*
> *And if everything you have is from God, why*
> *boast as though it were not a gift?"*
> *I Corinthians 4:7 (NLT)*

According to I Corinthians 4:7 (NLT), Christian businesses should be all about God and God alone.

The temptation to want to be in charge – to not let God be God – is great. It is a struggle that takes place every day. That is why Jesus calls us to carry our cross daily and follow Him.

When things are not going well, there is a very strong temptation to think *we* have to find the right strategy, do the right planning, and put the right people in place to ensure the company ends the year successfully in terms of profit and revenue. This is where Christian business owners err. To surrender and give up our personal rights is not a one-time event; it is a daily – sometimes hourly – occurrence. It is critical during downticks to acknowledge God's sovereignty and relinquish any control we *do* have to God.

God does hold us accountable to do the very best we can in terms of strategy, planning and forecasting. We must do everything necessary to present our best effort to God. But the next step is to be quiet and allow Him to direct our steps.

These fundamental beliefs set Christian business owners apart from those who do not believe in God. Christian business owners acknowledge that God directs our path. Proverbs 16:9 (NLT) reminds us that man may plan his way, but it is God who directs his path.

This Scripture is true not just in our personal lives, but also in the lives of our companies. I remember several different times in our ten-year history when we were on the brink of going under – we were about to lose 40% of our accounts or about to go bankrupt – and God was always the one who carried us out.

There are many things we can do as business owners to make our business better and to see it grow, but at the end of the day, we are not in charge of results. Results are never guaranteed. In fact, you could talk to any entrepreneur about results and he would say, "Yes, your results will stand a better chance if you plan and strategize well, but it is never a 100 percent guarantee." Some very well-known companies have put a great strategy in place and still gone bankrupt.

The flip side is also true. I have seen many nonprofits go under because they do not plan well. They simply think that they can sit in a room and just pray all day and have absolutely no business plan whatsoever. Scripture reminds us that man plans his way, but it will be God who directs his path. Planning and trusting go hand in hand. It is not one thing or the other.

These past two years I have had the privilege of attending an executive program for CEOs at Harvard Business School. [†††] Some may wonder, why do we need a secular institution to run a God-centered company? It is my deepest conviction that when God has gifted us with a talent, it is our job to hone it and refine it to the best of our ability. If God has granted someone the gift of singing, this person needs to practice and take lessons in order to offer God the best gift he or she is able to offer.

Harvard Business School has equipped me to be the best leader I can be. The skills, strategies and opportunities I have experienced at HBS have been invaluable to me as a CEO. To be able to trust God fully and to use the skills HBS has equipped me with is indeed experiencing the best of both worlds.

Another organization I had the chance to be part of is C-12. C-12 is a Christian organization geared for Christian CEOs. C-12 has been around for twenty-two years equipping Christian CEOs in leading their companies God's way. This great organization holds me accountable, trains me to lead a company God's way, and encourages me to faithfully learn from other CEOs who are in the group. We meet one day a month, and our meetings are always full of encouragement. I have learned so many valuable biblical lessons through C-12. We as CEOs should never have to lead alone. It does indeed seem lonely at times, but it does not have to be.

We serve an excellent God. We must treat God's gifts with distinction all of our lives. In the area of business, we must study hard, work hard, and trust God each step of the way. God will honor our faithfulness to the gift He has given us if we treat it with reverence and strive to improve each and every day.

The Apostle Paul was very strategic in the way he advanced the gospel. He did not just share Christ in any random place. He shared Christ where there is a vast stream of commerce so merchants and customers would trust Christ and go back to their own towns and share the good news of Jesus.

If you look at Jesus, he spent the first thirty years of His life preparing Himself for ministry. In three short years, he finished all that God had asked Him to accomplish. Can you imagine finishing everything in three years of our lives?

Jesus was also strategic. He heard the voice of His father and stayed the course and planned well. He trained the twelve disciples, and it was these twelve disciples who changed the world through the power of the Holy Spirit. So, at the end of the day, we must trust God. One reminder I frequently tell myself is: *I can either humble myself, or God will do it for me.* Humility comes when we are not successful, when we need to depend on God. I believe that God sometimes sends downticks or failure to Christian business owners as a reminder to be on our knees, to be in prayer, and to seek after Him.

There is a definite reason for every event that takes place, both in our personal life and the life of our business. Often times – and this has happened in my life, too – when things are not going well, we blame God. But, God remains in total control. God is sovereign. He is still the Father, the creator, and the God who loves us. He will never change.

So if God remains in total control, we must acknowledge that God is with us in our failures. In fact, it is through failing that we learn God is in control and that God is the only one who can pull us up out of failure.

The reason I entitled this chapter "It is All About God" is because there are many business owners who feel like they "do it alone," especially if they are the number one guy in the company. When you feel like there is no one you can turn to, at the end of the day, God is the one who will carry you and move you forward.

Indeed, it *is* all about God. It is my hope and my prayer that Christian business owners around the world will recognize God's sovereignty and allow God to lead their companies to great success.

QUESTIONS FOR REFLECTION

1. What is the difference between a Christian business person and a business person who is a Christian?

    _____

    _____

    _____

    _____

2. How do each of these perspectives differ when something goes wrong?

    _____

    _____

    _____

    _____

3. Do you believe that God owns your company? If so, why? If not, why not?

    _____

    _____

    _____

    _____

4. How do you incorporate Christian principles into

your company?

_____

_____

_____

_____

5. Where in your business is God currently providing direction?

_____

_____

_____

_____

6. On a scale of 1 to 10 (with 10 being "frequently)), how much and how often is God part of the decision making process in your business?

_____

_____

_____

_____

7. Give an example of a time when God blessed you in your life and/or business.

_____

_____

_____

_____

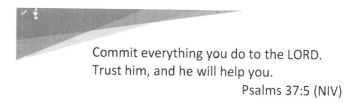

Commit everything you do to the LORD.
Trust him, and he will help you.

Psalms 37:5 (NIV)

FUTURE VISION

Christian CEOs seem to either rely so completely on God that they deliver very poor execution and strategies, or they contribute excellent skills and strategies but feel no need to rely on God's sovereignty.

I believe as Christian CEOs, we are responsible to deliver both. We must strategize, plan, market, and do everything humanly possible in the business realm. Then we must trust the Lord in the process, asking Him each step of the way whether we are doing His will or seeking our own desires. We need affirmation every step of the process.

How do we plan for the future while we, at the same time, trust God for the future? The best time to plan and strategize about the future is when the company is on an uptick.

When a company is going downhill – losing money, not doing well – is the worst time to think about the future because that is when humans tend to get nervous, hopeless, and begin making rash decisions instead of taking time to pray over them.

One of the things we have instituted at EIS Office Solutions is that every time we are on a business uptick, we plan and strategize about the future. We are very excited about the ministry God put before us in our most recent future planning sessions.

Very soon, we will be launching a brand new website and business called Secor. Through Secor, we will be selling mainly ink and toner. One hundred percent of the profit of Secor will be donated to ministries that are freeing girls from human sex trafficking here in the U.S. and around the world.

Human Sex Trafficking has now become the #1 crime in the world. Drug traffickers are changing their occupation because they said that they can only sell drugs one time and get a one-time profit, but a girl they can sell over and over again and get multiple profits throughout her life. That statement is so devastating yet so true. Recently, a Houston Police officer found a girl as young as five years old trapped in human sex trafficking. Can you imagine the atrocity of this sin? Can you imagine your own five-year-old daughter getting kidnapped and put into sex slavery? Sadly, many people see prostitution and immediately jump to the conclusion that these girls or women chose this path. The reality is that many girls involved in prostitution were either kidnapped or coerced into sex slavery.

In many of the Asian, Eastern Europe, and South American poverty-stricken countries, smugglers promise families that their daughters will have a job and a better life in the United States. After they arrive, they are sold into sex slavery until they are sixteen years old. Sadly, most of them commit suicide because the human body is just not capable of having sex 20 to 30 times a day as they are required to do by these ruthless people.

God laid it on our hearts in 2012 that our company needed to do something about child sex slavery, so we are doing the best we can to faithfully follow God and help these girls to be rescued in the name of Jesus.

We are asking God to grow this company exponentially nationwide. We want our customers' monies to support ministries in their own cities. For instance, if you are in San Francisco and you buy your ink and toner from Secor, you can donate your payment to the ministry in San Francisco. We will have ministry partners throughout the United States rescuing girls from human sex trafficking.

This particular future vision entered our planning sessions about a year ago when we were experiencing a period of rapid growth. We had won several large accounts, and we were able to really take our time to think about this. It has taken a year to pray over and plan Secor. August of this year is our target date to launch this new website business.

But how do we as Christians think about the future and plan at the same time? First and foremost is prayer. I believe prayer is the foundation of not just our everyday life, but every decision made by our companies. The future is in God's hands, and the prayer should be this: God, what do you want us to do in the future.

The second thing Christian business owners should begin to do is listen carefully to your management and team members. We have asked them to pray for the company. It should not surprise us if God chooses to send an answer through any member of the team. We asked God for the plan. He delivered the plan. Now we need to trust that plan.

For example, at EIS, we prayed for God to send us the next step, and God gave us the vision for Secor. Next, we began planning and strategizing what Secor would look like after the vision was given to us.

As we plan out each and every step, we're asking God, "God, is this what you want us to do?"

After we pray, we listen. After we listen, we begin implementing. And even in the implementing process, we ask God to confirm for us that what we are doing is right.

We never move ahead of God. We never implement a plan too quickly. We always take time to pray. We always take time to listen. Each step is prayed over and covered with prayer.

That is one thing that business people do so poorly; they move ahead of God. They tend to do their own thing instead of doing God's thing. We tend to do our thing and ask God's blessing on it; then, when it doesn't work, we blame it on God.

Decisions should actually be made in the reverse. We should ask God for direction. Once he has given us a direction, then we should plan and strategize.

And when a decision is made under the direction of God, there is rarely any anxiety. When a decision is made in God's timing, there is always peace because peace comes from the Lord. The Lord does not give anxiety. Anxiety comes from our flesh and from Satan. When we are anxious and unsure, we never move forward. Anxiety is a pretty clear indication of whether we're doing God's work or our own work. When we are doing God's work, we will always have peace. Even though it may be hard, we will sense God's hands on us.

So how do we hear God's voice and His calling? Just one word: intimacy. In a crowded room full of kids, I can pick out my daughter's voice and my son's voice. I know those voices because I am close to them. They are my son and my daughter. I can drown all the other kids' crying out because I am not close to them.

Every Godly man and woman I know spends intimate time with the Lord in His word, prayer, and worship. There is no shortcut to being intimate with God. The longer you spend time with him in the quietness of your soul, the more you can decipher whether it is your voice or God's voice.

I went to Dallas Theological Seminary (DTS) right out of college. DTS provided me with a great foundation that shaped my theology and calling in life. One thing I pounced on is the importance of God's Word and the way it transforms us. It is through spending regular time with God that we learn to distinguish His voice.

QUESTIONS FOR REFLECTION

1. How much quiet time do you spend with God each day?

   _____

   _____

   _____

   _____

2. What do you see as the benefits of spending time daily communicating with and listening to God?

   _____

   _____

   _____

   _____

3. If you truly believe God is who He says He is, how would that change your life and your business?

   _____

   _____

   _____

   _____

Our days on earth are like grass;
like wildflowers, we bloom and die.

Psalm 103:15 (NLT)

LIFE IS SHORT

There might be some people reading this book thinking they could never be an entrepreneur because they don't know how or they're afraid to try. I want to remind you that Scripture tells us our days on earth are numbered. We have a limited amount of time in which to make an impact on this world. If God is calling you to be an entrepreneur, then you must be faithful in fulfilling that call.

I am turning 40 this year. Sometime in my 20s I told God I would have absolutely no regret for the decisions I had made in my personal life or business relationships. I believe we must walk with God having that kind of mindset so we will be able to look back on every phase of our journey together without shame or remorse.

If there is no doubt God has placed the spirit of entrepreneurship in your heart, then your first reaction might be: This is going to be difficult. I don't know where to get the money. I don't know how to start.

I would encourage you, first and foremost, to do two things. First, write your plan out on paper – this is after confirming that, indeed, God wants you to be an entrepreneur. If God is leading you, then do this: write your plan on paper in as much detail as you can. It could be one page long. It could be fifty pages long. Whatever it is, write it down! What are you trying to sell? What service are you trying to offer? Just write down every idea God sends you on how you are going to grow this company. Put down any ideas that you may have on paper.

Secondly, seek counsel. Talk with other businessmen or men who have Christian businesses. Ask them for Godly counsel – Godly advice. They will give you a lot of ideas.

The first thing I did when I started EIS Office Solutions was to fly to Reno, Nevada and talk to a friend there who had started a business about ten years before. I just listened to his wisdom. I wrote everything I learned from him down on a piece of paper. That is how I first got started. Anything that was lacking, anything I didn't know, I would seek counsel. I continue to do the same to this day.

God has placed the body of believers all around us. It is not just for Sunday worship. It is for the fulfillment of God's kingdom. God wants to move His kingdom using the body of Christ. Christian entrepreneurs can make a huge impact on God's kingdom. The money we could donate and the time we could give to service with other ministries is tremendous. There's no other position that allows us to have more impact than as a Christian entrepreneur.

Granted, the first two, three, or four years of your business will be extremely difficult. You will spend significant hours growing your business. It is after that initial phase you find real freedom to do things for God's Kingdom, things you never thought possible. Remember, life is short. We want to be able to look back without regret, but, at the same time, we need to understand that one day we will die.

A few years ago I read an interview with retirees who were now in their 80s. Do you know what the number one regret they expressed was? They did not say that they wished they had worked more. It was not the amount of time or money they had spent. They did not say one thing that was worldly. They did say one thing that was very interesting though. They said they wished they had taken more risks.

Taking risks in life is one thing that is a huge barrier for us. Now, I am not talking about personal risk. I am talking about risks that God has given you and God wants you to take. There is a huge difference between taking a risk for your own glory and taking a risk for God's glory. I am strictly talking about something that is for God's glory – something God has put in your heart to expand His kingdom. We must do it because one day we will look back with full satisfaction when we hear God say, "Well done, good and faithful servant."

WORKS CITED

(n.d.). Retrieved from https://www.discprofile.com/what-is-disc/overview/dominance/

Evans, M. (2012, 08 30). *World Water Week : 26th - 31st August.* Retrieved 10 19, 2013, from Earth Times: http://www.earthtimes.org/going-green/world-water-week-26th-31st-august/2155/

Farlex Financial Dictionary. (2012). Retrieved 10 199, 2013, from <a href="http://financial-dictionary.thefreedictionary.com/Purchasing+price+parity">Purchasing Power Parity</a>

Global Issues. (Updated 2013, January 7). Retrieved 10 19, 2013, from Poverty Facts and Stats: http://www.globalissues.org/article/26/poverty-facts-and-stats

(2014). *Harvard Business School Case Studies.* 29: 04.

Johnson, A. (2013, 06 24). *76% of Americans are Living Paycheck to Paycheck.* Retrieved 10 19, 2013, from CNNMoney: http://money.cnn.com/2013/06/24/pf/emergency-savings/

Meeting the MDG Drinking Water and Sanitation Target - The Urban and Rural Challenge of the Decade. (2006). *World Health Organization and UNICEF Joint Program for Water Supply and Sanitation*, p. 47.

Random House Kernerman Webster's College Dictionary, © 2010 K Dictionaries Ltd. Copyright 2005, 1997, 1991 by Random House, Inc. All rights reserved. (2010). (Random House, Inc.) Retrieved October 12, 2013, from http://www.thefreedictionary.com/baptize: http://www.thefreedictionary.com/baptize

Romanet, I. (1988, November). *The Politics of Hunger*. Retrieved 10 19, 2013, from le Monde diplomatique (The English Edition): http://mondediplo.com/1998/11/01leader

United Nations. (2000, October 17). Retrieved 10 19, 2013, from International Day for the Eradication of Poverty: http://www.un.org/en/events/povertyday/2000/messages.htm

Wolfsensohn, J. (2012). The 9th International Anti-Corruption Conference. *Plenary Address.* Retrieved 10 19, 2013, from http://9iacc.org/papers/day1/plenary/d1pl_jwolfensohn.html

FOOTNOTES

[1] (Le Monde Diplomatique, 1998)

[*] (Global Issues, Updated 2013)

[†] (Meeting the MDG Drinking Water and Sanitation Target - The Urban and Rural Challenge of the Decade, 2006)

[‡] (Evans, 2012)

[§] http://www.ccainstitute.org/why-we-do-it-/facts-and-statistics.html (does this have parentheses around it like the other ones)

[**] which occur when we are sleeping

[††] which can occur when we are awake or asleep

[‡‡] http://online.wsj.com/news/articles/SB10000872396390443720204578004980476429190

[§§] http://mashable.com/2013/02/04/why-startups-fail/

[***] https://www.discprofile.com/what-is-disc/overview/dominance/

[†††] http://www.macmillandictionary.com/dictionary/american/leadership#leadership_6

[‡‡‡] (OPM 46)